Learn about Nature

Activity Book

Learn about Nature Activity Book

35 forest-school projects and adventures
for children aged 7 years +

CICO Kidz

This edition published in 2022 by CICO Books
An imprint of Ryland Peters & Small Ltd
20–21 Jockey's Fields   341 E 116th St
London WC1R 4BW   New York, NY 10029

First published in 2013 as *My First Nature Activity Book*

www.rylandpeters.com

10 9 8 7 6 5 4 3 2 1

A CIP catalog record for this book is available from the Library of Congress and the British Library.

ISBN: 978 1 80065 094 7

Printed in China

Series consultant: Susan Akass
Editors: Susan Akass, Katie Hardwicke
Designer: No Days Off, Barbara Suñiga
Step artworks: Rachel Boulton
Animal artworks: Hannah George
For photography credits, see page 128.

Art director: Sally Powell
Head of production: Patricia Harrington
Publishing manager: Penny Craig
Publisher: Cindy Richards

Contents

Introduction

Nature is wonderful! We all enjoy watching things grow or getting outside into the yard, the park, or into wild places. There's so much to see and do, so much to explore, and so many interesting things to collect. This book is full of great ideas that will make you even more fascinated by nature and which will get you outside even more often, by showing you exciting projects for making, doing, and growing.

In this book there are four chapters: In the Garden—which is full of fun projects to start you gardening and to make your garden more wildlife-friendly; Growing Fun—with great ideas for growing things inside your home or just outside on a doorstep or windowsill; The Outdoors Indoors—which is packed with craft projects using bits and pieces you can pick up on woodland walks or at the seaside; and finally, Outdoor Crafts and Games—which gives you ideas for all kinds of different games and activities to do while you are out and about in the great outdoors.

Most of these projects are very simple and use very few special materials but, to help you know where to start, we have graded them with one, two, or three smiley faces. The grade one projects are simple, quick, and use materials that you are likely to have in your craft cupboard. Grade two projects are a little more difficult, take a little longer, and may need materials that you will have to buy specially. Projects with three smiley faces are more challenging and require special equipment or materials.

Take a look at the Collecting Materials section (see pages 8—9) for ideas on what to look for and when. Getting Started (see pages 10—13) will also give you some useful tips and instructions for skills such as tying knots, planting seeds, and keeping safe. So get outside, get making, and have fun!

Project levels

Level 1

These are quick, easy projects that can be made with materials in your craft cupboard.

Level 2

These projects take a little longer and may need some special materials.

Level 3

These projects require special materials and may need help from an adult.

Collecting materials

Whenever you are out and about, keep your eyes peeled for suitable crafting materials. You will be amazed at the variety of natural treasures you can collect right outside your back door throughout the year.

When you are out and about Think Green!

- Always respect nature.
- Only take things from the ground, try not to damage living plants.
- Never take living creatures out of their environment.
- If you turn over rocks or logs put them back how you found them and watch out for bugs or wildlife that may be hiding underneath.
- Be careful when you pick berries, nuts, or fruit as these can be poisonous—always check with an adult before you collect them.
- Watch out for bugs—wasps feed on fallen fruit and take care not to disturb wasp, bee, or ant nests.
- Never touch mushrooms and fungi as these are often deadly poisonous, and make sure that you are aware of any plants that should not be touched, like poison ivy—always ask an adult if you're not sure.
- Take all your litter home with you.
- Close all gates so farm animals don't escape from fields.
- Always take care near water—never enter water to fetch a boat or twig that has blown out of reach.

What to collect and when

Remember always to wash your hands well after you have been outside collecting, making, or playing.

Winter When the trees and hedgerows are bare, look out for pieces of bark, interesting shaped twigs and dried out seed heads.

Spring and Summer Enjoy the wild flowers and fresh green leaves. Most wild flowers should be left to grow where they are, but you could pick a few common ones like buttercups and daisies and some pretty grasses or beautiful fronds of ferns and other leaves. (You could also ask permission to pick some garden flowers.) Use them fresh for some projects or take them inside and dry them to use later. Dry them by hanging them in a warm, dry place, or press them between pieces of paper, under a pile of books, or in a flower press.

Fall (Autumn) This is the best season to go foraging—whether for blackberries for a blackberry and apple pie or for colored leaves and all the many different types of seeds you can use in your craft projects.

All year round Evergreen trees can provide you with pine cones and interesting leaves to use on printing projects and for your homemade paper (see page 84), while shells, pebbles, driftwood, and sea glass can be gathered at the beach whatever the season.

Foraging essentials

When you go out always dress for the conditions:
- In winter—wear warm clothes, a waterproof jacket, and rain/wellie boots (so you can tramp through dirt and puddles)
- In summer—wear long trousers and trainers (so you don't get scratched or stung by nettles) and a sun hat and sun block (so you don't get burnt)
- All year round—take a waterproof jacket for unexpected showers!

Don't forget to bring something to carry your finds in—a pail (bucket), a basket, or a plastic bag will do fine. Egg cartons are good for putting small finds in to keep them safe. A back pack will keep your hands free for climbing and exploring.

Reusing and recycling

People who care about nature reuse and recycle.

Check your garden and shed for:
- Old terra-cotta flower pots and saucers
- Roofing tiles
- Pieces of timber
- Worn out rain boots/wellies
- A broken wheelbarrow
- Lengths of twine
- Almost finished pots of paint
- Old potting mix (compost) bags

All of these are used in different projects in this book.

Check your house for:
- Empty jars for storing your finds such as seeds, shells, and small pebbles
- Old newspapers—essential for covering the work surfaces while you craft
- Old gift wrap as it often comes in great patterns and colors
- Tissue paper
- Computer print outs unused on one side
- Cardboard boxes—shoeboxes, cereal packets, egg cartons, etc—these are good for storing your finds in
- Scraps of fabrics and ribbons
- Fruit such as melons and mangoes—remind your family to keep the skins whole when they peel them so you can make fruity boats (see page 96)

Getting started with crafting

For the projects in this book collect what you can from nature, and reuse and recycle bits and pieces from your house or backyard and shed. You will also need a store of craft materials to get you going. These are the basics:

Glue

- PVA is suitable for most projects in the book. It is safe and easy to use, but can be messy so make sure that you cover your work surface with newspaper before you start. It takes a little while to dry, so be patient.
- Glue sticks are good for sticking paper together but are not strong enough for heavier materials.
- Modeling clay is useful for attaching things together that may not stick well with glue, such as twigs, conkers, and seeds.

Paint

- Poster paints are good for crafting because they are nontoxic and washable. For a basic kit, buy red, yellow, and blue, which can be mixed together to create lots more colors, and white and black to lighten and darken them.
- Get a selection of inexpensive paintbrushes in different sizes. Always wash them well after use.
- Paper plates are good for mixing paints on. Use old yogurt pots for paint and glue.
- For some projects you will need water-based latex (emulsion) house paint and varnish. Try to use pots left over from decorating but always ask first.
- Acrylic pens are an easy way of adding fine details to decorations.

String

- Nothing is more useful than a piece of string. For these nature activities try to use string made from natural fibers such as raffia, jute, and sisal which will eventually rot away if left outside.
- When you are out and about try using natural materials such as long grasses, reeds, or climbing plants, such as vines, to bind sticks together.

Scissors and knives

- For many of these craft activities you will need strong sharp scissors—always be careful when using or carrying them.
- As you get older you may be allowed a pen knife when you are out in the wild. Make sure that you are taught how to use it properly, always cutting away from you or down onto a firm surface.

Blowing eggs

If you'd like to keep your Leaf print Easter eggs (see page 80), then it is a good idea to blow the egg first. You can use blown eggs for other craft projects, too.

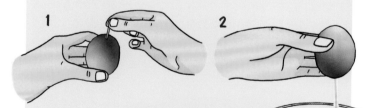

1 You may need to ask an adult to help. Using a needle, prick a small hole in one end of the egg and a slightly larger hole at the other end.

2 Push the needle into the egg and prod it around to break the yolk. Holding the egg over a small bowl, blow (don't suck!) through the small hole. The egg yolk and white will come out through the larger hole into the bowl.

3 Place the empty eggshell under running water to gently clean the inside.

Other useful techniques

Tying a strong knot and braiding (plaiting) string can come in useful when you're out and about, in the garden, or making something at home.

Reef knot

This is a strong knot to tie two pieces of string together or to tie two ends together to make a loop.

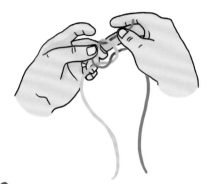

1 Take the left end of the string, pass it across the right end and twist it underneath.

2 The ends have now swapped places. Take what has now become the right end and pass it over the left end, twist it underneath, and bring it up through the loop you have just made.

3 Now pull all the ends tight.

4 This little rhyme will help you remember: "Left over right and under, right over left and under."

Braiding (plaiting)

This makes a strong length of twine or string that can be used for hanging heavier things, like the bird feeder on page 20.

1 Knot three equal pieces of twine or wool together at one end. Hold the knotted end firm with a bulldog clip, stick it down with some tack, or put a heavy book on top (or ask someone to hold it for you).

2 Take the right strand over the middle strand—this then becomes the middle strand.

3 Take the left strand over the middle strand – this then becomes the middle strand.

4 Keep repeating right over middle, left over middle, until you reach the end. Tie the strands together in a knot.

Getting started in the garden

Some of the projects involve growing plants. Here are a few guidelines to help you to sow seeds and look after your growing plants, so that your flowers, herbs, and vegetables are healthy and strong.

Gardening materials

- Hand trowel
- Hand fork
- Garden scissors
- Watering can
- Garden twine
- Bamboo canes
- Gardening gloves
- Rain boots/wellies
- Suitable clothing that you don't mind getting covered in dirt
- Potting mix (compost)
- Gravel
- Plant pots and containers

Garden safety

- Wear a pair of gardening gloves whenever handling soil or material like well-rotted compost in the garden. This will prevent you picking up harmful bacteria.

- Don't eat anything without asking permission and washing it first.

- Always wash your hands after you've been gardening.

- Don't pick leaves, flowers, or berries without asking permission first—some garden plants are poisonous.

Growing seeds

You can buy seeds in packets from a garden center or collect your own from seed heads in the garden to plant the following year. (Check that the seeds aren't poisonous.)

To plant seeds in a pot or container:

1 Fill the container with potting mix (compost).
2 Firm it down gently to leave a level surface.
3 Scatter the seeds thinly on top.
4 Cover with soil or potting mix— about ½ inch (1 cm) deep for most small seeds.
5 Water and put them in a warm, light place to germinate.

- If you are planting seeds inside, to help the seeds germinate you can make a mini greenhouse by placing a clear plastic freezer bag over the pot and securing it with an elastic band. Remove it after the seeds have germinated.

- If you have planted seeds in the container they are going to grow in, you may need to thin them out a little so that they have room to grow. Check the seed packet for how big the spaces should be and pull out the weaker seedlings until there are big enough gaps between the plants that are left.

Scattering the seeds

Thinning out seedlings

Planting out

When planting into a container, or directly into the soil in the garden, you need to prepare the plant and dig a hole.

1 Make sure that you give the plant a good drink of water in its pot about an hour before you begin planting.
2 Prepare your planting hole by digging a space twice as wide as the plant pot, forking over the bottom and giving it a good watering.
3 Take your plant carefully out of its pot, place it in the hole, making sure it is planted at the same depth as it was in the pot.
4 Push the soil back into the spaces around it and firm the soil down well.
5 Then give it another good watering.

Watering

Plants need a lot of water to keep them healthy, especially when they are young or newly-planted and when the weather is warm and dry.

- You will need to water small seedlings and plants in pots almost every day if the weather is dry.
- The best time to water is early morning and evening because less water will evaporate in the sun in this way—but if you see your plants wilting and drooping in the heat, then don't wait!
- For larger plants, such as climbing beans, which you have planted into the ground, a thorough watering once a week is better than a little bit every day, because it will make the plant grow longer deeper roots.
- Try to have a watering can with a fine rose (the part with holes at the end of the spout) so that it pours a very gentle shower. This is less likely to wash away small seedlings. You can also water seed trays and plant pots by standing them in a bowl of

shallow water for 15–30 minutes (the larger the pot, the longer you leave it).

Tying-in

Tie plants to a cane with a figure eight. Take the twine twice round the cane, twist it and then tie it loosely around the plant stem.

Plant ideas

If you've caught the gardening bug and want to grow and plant different plants in containers, or in the garden, you may be finding it difficult to decide what to grow. To make choosing easier, here are themed lists of some fun and exciting plants. Whether you've got a large garden or yard, or just a window box, there are some great plants to try.

Salad-bowl garden

- Lettuce 'Lollo Rosso'
- Spinach 'Bordeaux' (red stem, baby leaf)
- Lettuce 'Mizuna'
- Scallion/Spring onion
- Cherry tomato 'Tumbler'
- Cucumber
- Lettuce 'Little Gem'
- Edible carrot leaf (grown for leaves, not roots)
- Mustard
- Radish
- Beet/Beetroot 'Bulls Blood' (grown for its leaves)
- Tatsoi

Crazy fruit and vegetables

- Brussels sprouts 'Red Delicious' (purple sprouts)
- Chard 'Bright Lights' (mix of white, red, pink, gold, and orange stems)
- Strawberry 'Maxim' (fruit as big as a small hand)
- Tomato 'Tigerella' (stripy fruit)
- Squash 'Turks Turban'
- Borlotti bean 'Lamon' (pink and white blotched pods and mottled beans)
- French bean 'Purple King' (dwarf purple beans)
- Cucumber 'Crystal Lemon' (round, yellow fruit)
- Eggplant/Aubergine 'Mohican' (white fruit)
- Carrot 'Purple Haze' (purple carrots)
- Sweetcorn 'Indian Summer' (white, red, purple, and yellow kernels on the same cob)
- Sweetcorn 'Red Strawberry' (for popcorn)
- Raspberry 'Allgold' (golden raspberries)
- Beet/Beetroot 'Chioggia' (cut it open to reveal white and red concentric rings)
- Zucchini/Courgette 'One Ball' (round, orange fruit)

Fast-growing seeds

- Radish
- Carrot 'Parmex'
- Arugula/Rocket
- Cress
- Spinach
- Turnip 'Arcoat'
- Beet/Beetroot 'Pronto'
- Nigella 'Miss Jekyll' (love-in-a-mist)
- Limnanthes (poached egg plant)
- Nasturtium
- Eschscholzia (California poppy)
- Cerinthe major (honeywort)
- Cosmidium
- Sunflowers
- Annual poppies (not opium poppy)

Scratch and sniff

- Stachys byzantina (lamb's ears)
- Salvia officinalis 'Icterina' (variegated sage)
- Salvia argentea (woolly leaves)
- Bergenia (elephant's ears)
- Stipa tenuissima (feather grass)
- Melianthus major (blue leaves that smell of peanut butter)
- Briza maxima (quaking grass)
- Thyme
- Basil
- Antennaria (catsfoot)
- Helichrysum italicum 'Serotinum' (curry plant)
- Bellis perennis (daisy)
- Callistemon (bottlebrush)
- Convolvulus cneorum (soft, silver leaves)
- Coprosma (shiny, glossy leaves)
- Bronze fennel (feathery foliage)

Giant's garden

- Musa basjoo (hardy banana)
- Hosta 'Big Daddy'
- Bamboo
- Tree fern
- Fatsia japonica
- Cardoon
- Melianthus major
- Tetrapanax papyrifer (rice paper plant)
- Pole/Runner beans
- Macleaya cordata (plume poppy)
- Verbena bonariensis
- Helianthus 'Lemon Queen'
- Dahlia imperialis (tree dahlia)
- x Fatshedera lizei

Plants for pots

- Pansies and violets
- Petunia
- Begonia
- Nasturtium
- Sempervivum (houseleeks)
- Marigold
- Pelargonium
- Cosmos atrosanguineus (chocolate cosmos)
- Fuchsia
- Brassica oleracea (ornamental cabbage)
- Lagurus ovatus (hare's tail grass)
- Solenostemon (coleus)
- Pennisetum 'Purple Majesty'
- Heathers
- Box topiary shapes

Nature's garden

- Buddleja (butterfly bush)
- Hebe
- Veronica
- Leucanthemum vulgare (oxeye daisy)
- Pole/Runner beans
- Dipsacus fullonum (teasel)
- Forget-me-not
- Stipa tenuissima (feather grass)
- Sunflower
- Lavender
- Marigold
- Nepeta (catmint/catnip)
- Fennel
- Sedum spectabile
- Marjoram
- Rosemary
- Thyme
- Chives

What not to grow

Many well-known garden plants are poisonous, have vicious spikes, or are covered in tiny hairs, which cause irritation to the skin when touched. These plants should be avoided.

- Aconitum (monkshood)
- Alstroemeria
- Brugmansia (angel's trumpet)
- Castor oil plant
- Delphinium
- Echium (viper's bugloss)
- Euphorbia
- Foxglove
- Giant hogweed
- Laburnum
- Lupin(e)
- Nerium oleander (oleander)
- Rue
- Solanum
- Zantedeschia (calla lily)

In the Garden

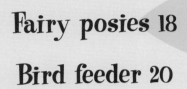

Fairy posies

Most flowers should be left just where they are—growing in the country or in a garden for the bees and butterflies to enjoy and so they can make seeds for new flowers. However, as these tiny posies only need a few flowers, it is fine to make them to decorate your dolls' tea parties or as little gifts for special visitors.

You will need

....

Sprigs of tiny assorted flowers

A medium-sized leaf

Scissors

Raffia or ribbon for a bow

1 Pick an assortment of tiny flowers, such as daisies, from your yard or garden and a medium-sized plain leaf in which to wrap them.

2 Arrange the flowers on the leaf and fold the leaf around the stems of the flowers to hold them in place.

Tiny POSIES make SPECIAL GIFTS!

3 Cut a length of raffia to tie around the posy. Wrap the raffia around the base of the leaf and tie in a neat bow. Trim the ends of the raffia with scissors.

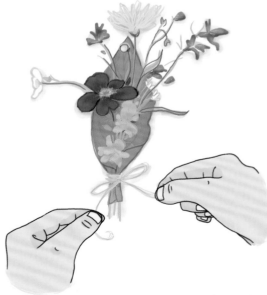

Bird feeder

Wild birds in your garden will flock to visit this colorful bird feeder. You can make it around the time of Halloween when there are plenty of pumpkins in the stores or your garden, and the birds are beginning to get hungry. Decorate it with cloves and fill it with lovely, sticky bird cake. Hang it from a tree outside your window and watch the birds tuck in!

You will need

A small pumpkin

A large spoon

A toothpick (cocktail stick) or wooden skewer for piercing holes in the pumpkin

Dried cloves

Scissors

String

A small nail

1 packet of lard, at room temperature

A large mixing bowl

Good quality birdseed (about twice the volume of the lard)

You can add all sorts of other ingredients to your bird cake mix to make it more attractive to birds—try oatmeal, cheese, peanuts, and dried fruit.

1 Ask an adult to cut the pumpkin in half. Pull out all the seed from one half with your hands and carve away the flesh from the inside with a large spoon. Now use the toothpick or skewer to make a hole near to the rim of the pumpkin and push in a clove. Make a design of cloves right around the rim of the pumpkin.

2 Now make the hanging loop. Cut six 3-foot (1-m) long pieces of string. Take three strands and knot them together at one end. Start braiding (plaiting) the string (see page 11)—it's easier if you slip the knot under something heavy to hold it firm, stick it down with some tack, or ask someone to hold it for you. When you reach the end knot it again. Braid the other three lengths to make the second hanging loop.

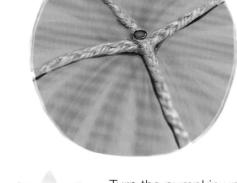

3 Turn the pumpkin upside down. Lay the braided string in an "X" across the base. Push or hammer in a nail to hold the string in place.

4 Leave the lard out of the refrigerator until it is soft. Cut it up into small pieces and put it into a large bowl. Add some birdseed and mix it into the lard with your finger tips. Keep adding the seed and mixing until the fat holds it all together. (This is a very messy activity!) Spoon the mixture into the pumpkin bowl.

5  Tie the ends of the string around a branch of a tree, where you can see it from your window. (You might need to ask a tall adult to help you.) If necessary, trim the ends using scissors. You can make a second feeder with the other half of the pumpkin.

Wheelbarrow veg garden

You don't need lots of space, or even a yard or garden, to grow tasty vegetables. Using an old wheelbarrow and some seeds and plants that won't grow too big, you can create a mobile mini vegetable plot. Choose quick-growing vegetables and, as the wheelbarrow isn't very deep, choose only very small varieties of root vegetables.

You will need

An old wheelbarrow

A scrubbing brush

Warm, soapy water

Gravel or stones

Potting mix (compost)

Water-retaining granules

Garden twine or string

Clothes pins (pegs)

A selection of dwarf or compact seed species or small plants, such as:

1 mini fava (broad) bean plant, 1 cherry tomato plant, beets (beetroot) seed, 'Tom Thumb' lettuce seeds, 'Parmex' carrot seeds, radish seeds

Short sticks or bamboo canes

A watering can with a fine rose

1 In late spring, when there is no danger of frost, wheel your wheelbarrow to a sunny place where it won't be in anyone's way. Ask an adult to drill or puncture holes every 4–6 inches (10–15 cm) in the base of the wheelbarrow. Use the scrubbing brush and warm, soapy water to give the wheelbarrow a good clean, and then let it dry. Add a layer of gravel, about ¾–1¼ inches (2–3 cm) deep, to the bottom of the wheelbarrow to help with drainage.

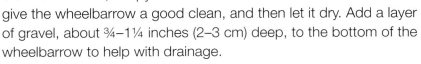

2 In a separate tub or pail (bucket), mix some water-retaining granules into some potting mix then add this to the wheelbarrow so that it comes to within 1¾–2 inches (4–5 cm) of the top.

3 Cut one length of garden twine or string a little longer than the length of your wheelbarrow. Knot the ends, position the twine down the center of the barrow, and secure the ends to the rim with clothes pins (pegs). Cut two more lengths a little longer than the width and attach them across the width to mark out six square sections over the top of the wheelbarrow—these will make mini fences.

4 Sow or plant a different type of seed or plant in each square (see page 12). Place the tallest plants (the beans and tomatoes) at the deeper end of the wheelbarrow, so that their roots have more room to grow. Plant the smaller ones (the lettuce and radish) in the shallower section.

5 Plants such as tomatoes and beans may grow quite tall, so push a short stick or bamboo cane into the potting mix next to these plants so that you can tie them in as they grow taller (see page 13).

6 Water the plants well, using the fine rose on the end of your watering can so that you don't disturb the potting mix around the seeds. Keep the barrow well watered.

7 When the seeds have grown into seedlings about ½ inch (1 cm) tall, you may need to thin them out so that they have more room to grow (see page 12). Check on the seed packet to see how far apart the seedlings should be and pull out some seedlings to leave spaces between them.

8 Harvest your vegetables when they're fully grown— radishes will be the first to be ready. Eat and enjoy!

A BARROWFUL of FUN and FLAVOR!

Wooden nesting box

You could put a plain wooden nesting box up in your garden or you could transform it into you very own designer residence that any bird would be proud to nest in. Use matte latex (emulsion) wall paint and then varnish the box to protect it, or you could use water-based exterior wood paint for this project.

You will need

A plain wooden nesting box

Large and small paintbrushes

Water-based undercoat

Pastel-green colored paint—either matte latex (emulsion) or water-based exterior wood paint

Cream matte latex (emulsion) or water-based exterior wood paint

About 6 standard-size wooden popsicle/craft sticks for picket fence

About 16 large wooden popsicle/craft sticks (depending on size of box) for roof

PVA glue or all-purpose adhesive and glue brush

Strong scissors

Water-based acrylic varnish (if you have used matte latex/emulsion paint)

1 Use a large paintbrush to paint the nesting box with undercoat. Paint the bottom first and let it dry before turning it over and painting all over the rest of it. Let it dry completely. Always wash your brush well after you have finished painting.

2 Once the undercoat is dry, paint the box all over with green paint except the roof. Let it dry. Paint on another coat of green paint, if the paint looks patchy, and let it dry thoroughly.

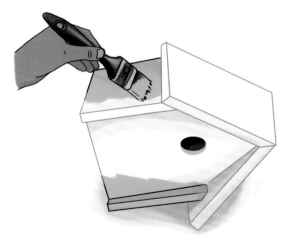

3 Using a smaller paintbrush, paint undercoat on one side and the edges of all the popsicle sticks. Let them dry. When they are dry, turn them over and paint undercoat on the other side. Let them dry again.

4 When they are dry, paint one side only of all of the small sticks and eight of the large sticks with cream paint. Wash your brush and then paint the other eight large sticks green. Let them dry. Paint another coat, if the paint looks patchy.

5 Spread glue all over the backs of the large craft sticks and stick them to one side of the roof. Glue them in alternate colors to create a striped effect. Prop the house up so that this side of the roof is horizontal and the sticks don't slide off as they dry. Let them dry before doing the other side.

6 Cut four of the smaller popsicle sticks in half, using strong scissors, to make the picket fence. Lay them along the base of the front of the nesting box and glue them in an even row along this edge, leaving a gap between each stick.

7 Glue the two whole smaller popsicle sticks horizontally along the top and bottom of the picket fence. If you have used matte latex (emulsion) paint, finish the nesting box with one or two coats of varnish to make it suitable for outdoor use.

Insect hotel

Minibeasts are really important in your yard or garden and you can help them by building this multistory insect hotel to give them somewhere to shelter and hide in. You'll find it soon fills up with lots of garden visitors, from bees and ladybugs to lacewings and woodlice.

You will need

24 old bricks

Old curved roof tiles

10 short pieces of timber (wood) of about the same length

Materials to fill the hotel, such as corrugated cardboard, bamboo canes, drinking straws, old pots, logs, egg cartons, pine cones, and dry leaves

A selection of hollow tubes (including empty cardboard tubes and plastic pipes or bottles)

If curved tiles are hard to find, you could use overlapping flat ones on the top to keep the rain out, or even a piece of roofing felt or corrugated plastic.

1

Find a quiet, sheltered spot in the garden and make sure that the ground is flat. Build one wall that is two bricks long and two bricks high. Use the length of one of your pieces of timber to measure where the second wall should be. The wood will need to rest across the two walls.

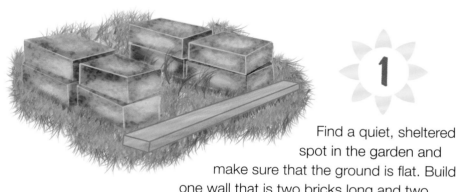

2

Put a curved roof tile between the two rows of bricks to provide a shelter for toads and frogs. (If you haven't got any curved roof tiles, half bury a flower pot in the soil, leaving a small entrance.) Lay three pieces of timber, spaced at equal distances, across the rows of bricks. Add another one or two rows of bricks and some more timber in order to build up the storys.

3 On the top story, add three more pieces of timber, with an extra piece of timber at the back of the stack. This will make the tiles tip forward, which will help the rain run off. Place the tiles on top overlapping their edges to make a roof.

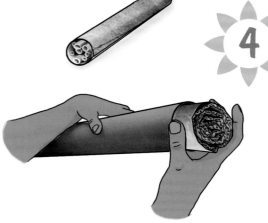

4 Now fill up your hotel with all sorts of materials to provide nooks and crannies for minibeasts to hide in—roll up pieces of corrugated cardboard so that you can slide them inside the old cardboard tubes. Put the filled tubes inside the hotel and then fill the other cardboard tubes and plastic pipes with a selection of hollows stems, such as sections of bamboo and drinking straws.

5 Ask an adult to drill holes in the ends of logs to include in your hotel. Then add other materials like old egg cartons, pine cones, twigs, and dry leaves.

6 Finally, find a flat tile or piece of slate and write the name of your hotel on it with chalk or acrylic paint pens.

A four-star HOTEL for your GARDEN FRIENDS!

Pebble birdbath

Lots of people put out food for birds but forget that they need to drink and have baths as well. Make this pebbly birdbath, place it on a low wall or table, and you will be able to watch the birds splashing around outside your window. When you go to the beach you can collect small pretty pebbles or you can buy specially polished ones.

You will need

Paintbrush

Gray masonry paint

Terra-cotta pot saucer about 14 inches (35 cm) in diameter

A selection of pebbles in assorted colors

A large wooden craft stick

A pot of waterproof grout and adhesive with spreader

A damp sponge and bowl of water

1 Using a thick paintbrush, paint the whole outside of the saucer. Let it dry then turn it over and paint the inside rim. Let that dry thoroughly too.

2 Arrange the pebbles on the base of the saucer in a pretty design. Use pebbles that are a similar size and not too big. Take time to work out your pattern.

WATCH the birds SPLASH!

3 Pick up one of the pebbles and apply a dab of the grout to the base of it, using the end of a large wooden craft stick. Replace the pebble on the saucer exactly where you took it from. Press the pebble gently in place, without using too much pressure.

4 One by one, stick the rest of the pebbles to the saucer with the grout—work carefully to make sure that you haven't missed any! Let the birdbath dry completely overnight.

5 Now the messy part—use a plastic spreader (one usually comes in the pot of grout) to smooth the grout over the pebbles and the whole base of the saucer. Use the craft stick to push the grout down between the pebbles. The grout should reach right to the top of the pebbles.

6 Now use a damp sponge to smooth the surface of the grout and wipe as much grout as possible from the tops of the pebbles. Keep rinsing out your sponge as you do this. As the grout dries, sponge it again to remove any grout that is left. When almost dry, use a damp sponge to wipe the surface, and when completely dry, use a cloth to polish the pebbles and remove any grout dust.

Seed bombs

Are there places near you that are dull and boring and need some flowers to brighten them up? Seed bombs are a perfect way to introduce colorful wildflowers into corners of your town or city that nobody cares about. The clay protects the seeds from being eaten by birds, and when the seeds begin to grow, they break through the clay.

You will need

1 cup of air-drying modeling clay

A container for mixing

1 cup of potting mix (compost)

2 packets of native wildflower seeds (these flowers come up in the summer so this is an activity for the spring—the seeds need to be planted from March to May, when the weather begins to warm up)

A tray or baking sheet

1 Break the clay into small pieces then put it into a mixing bowl along with the potting mix and a splash of water. Rub the clay into the compost with your hands or a fork until the two are well combined. This can be a messy job so make sure there is a bowl of soapy water nearby for a quick clean-up afterward.

2 Sprinkle a couple of packets of wildflower seeds into your clay and potting mix mixture and gently stir them in with a fork.

BRIGHTEN up your NEIGHBORHOOD!

3 Roll your mixture into small, walnut-sized balls between your palms and put them on a tray or baking sheet. Put the tray of seed bombs on a sunny windowsill to dry out. This usually takes 24–48 hours.

Make sure you use a seed mix native to the country in which you live!

4 Take a bag of bombs out with you when you go for a walk and drop a few in uncared-for but sunny places where there is grass already growing or where there is bare soil. Come back in the summer to see if your flowers have grown.

Peanut heart

Birds love peanuts, especially in the winter months when there's not much food around. Unshelled peanuts can be pierced and threaded on wire to create bird feeders. A heart shape is shown here, finished with a raffia bow to make a pretty gift, but you can choose your own shape—birds aren't fussy!

You will need

Unshelled peanuts

Wooden skewer

Strong wire, about 30 inches (76 cm) long

Raffia for bow

Twine for hanging loop

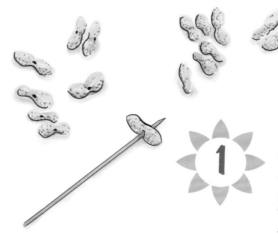

1 First, pierce the holes in the nuts using a wooden skewer. Be careful not to prick yourself! You may want to ask an adult to help. You will need about 60 peanuts for one peanut heart.

2 Fold the wire in half to create the "V" shape of the base of the heart. Begin threading peanuts onto the wire. Each side needs about 30 peanuts.

BIRDS will love this TREAT!

3

Bend each side of the heart into a curve to form a heart shape and twist the wire together to secure the ends in place. You may need to ask an adult with a pair of pliers to help you with this, if your wire is quite thick.

4

Now tie a raffia bow at the top of the heart to cover the wire ends. Cut an 8-inch (20-cm) length of twine to make a hanging loop. Hang the feeder from a tree branch and watch the birds come and find the nuts in the shells.

Climbing bean archway

With a few "magic" beans, you can rival Jack and his beanstalk and create this stunning archway. Watch as the bean seeds sprout and then race up to the top of the bamboo canes in just a few short weeks. Not only will your bean plants give you pretty flowers and delicious beans, but you can also use the archway to create an impressive entrance to a vegetable garden or play area.

You will need

Paper and a pencil

Card

Scissors

2 tall terra-cotta plant pots, at least 10 inches (25 cm) in diameter

Newspaper

Masking tape

Green matte latex (emulsion) paint

Large and small paintbrushes

White acrylic paint pen

Gravel or small stones

Potting mix (compost)

A watering can

4 x 6 ft (180 cm) bamboo canes

Garden twine or string

Pole/Runner beans or green bean seeds (climbing French beans)

1 Draw a leaf and a bean pod shape on a piece of paper. Cut out the shapes and use them as a template to draw round on two pieces of card. Starting in the middle of the shape, carefully cut out leaf- and bean-shaped holes to form your stencils.

2 Place the first pot on some newspaper and use the masking tape to position one stencil on the pot. Paint over the pattern with the green paint using the large paintbrush. Let the paint dry, unpeel the masking tape, and move the stencil to a new position (or use the other stencil). In this way continue to paint pods and leaves over both pots.

Make a GRAND entrance to your GARDEN!

3 Use the green paint and the small paintbrush to add the stems and tendrils that link the bean leaves and pods. Add veins and other fine details with the white acrylic paint pen.

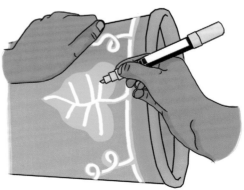

In late spring, when there is no danger of frost, it is time to plant your beans. Place your pots where you want the archway to be (this needs to be somewhere quite sunny) and then put some gravel or stones in the bottom of each one. Fill them to the top with potting mix, firming it down as you go. Water them well with the watering can.

Push two bamboo canes into each pot on opposite sides of the pot. Tie them together tightly at the top with string or twine—you may need help to reach!

Next, tie the two pairs of canes together to form the central point of the archway.

7 Now for the planting. With your finger, make a hole in the potting mix next to one of the canes. The hole should be three times deeper than the beans are wide. Drop the bean in the hole, cover it over, and firm down the potting mix. Do this again on the other side of the cane, so that you will have two bean plants for each cane. Repeat for the other three canes.

8 Beans like plenty of water, so water your pots almost every day. Watch to see when the beans germinate. When the plants are 4 or 5 inches (10–12 cm) tall, gently tie the stems to the canes using twine or string in a figure-eight knot (see page 13). This will help them start climbing and stop the stems rubbing on the cane and damaging the plant. As the bean plants grow, they will twist around the canes until they reach the top, creating a leafy archway.

Pick the beans regularly when they start to appear because this encourages the plant to produce more.

Chapter 2
Growing Fun

Tiny terrarium

An aquarium has water and fish in it (aqua means water), a terrarium has earth and plants in it (terra means earth). So, a terrarium is a garden in a large glass jar! They are fun to make, need very little watering or care, and look great on a windowsill or shelf.

You will need

A large glass container (we used a Mason jar)

Clay pellets

Horticultural charcoal

Potting mix (compost)

A long-handled spoon

A selection of suitable plants for your container, such as creeping fig, parlor palm, prayer plant, creeping Jenny, polka dot plant, and mind-your-own-business; avoid succulents, cacti, and plants grown for flowers

A watering can

1 Carefully wash your jar with detergent and water so that the glass is nice and clean and then rinse it. Dry it well. Slowly pour in the clay pellets to make a 2-inch (5-cm) drainage layer covering the base of the jar.

2 Permanently damp soil can become smelly, so add a thin layer of horticultural charcoal over the clay pellets, which will keep it fresh.

3 Fill a quarter of the container with potting mix and firmly press it down with your fingers (if your hand can't fit through the neck of the jar, use the back of a long-handled spoon to press the soil down).

4 This is the fun but fiddly part—use the long-handled spoon to dig out small planting holes and lower the plants into position. Firm the soil around the root balls with the spoon. When you have finished planting, drop in some more clay pellets to fill any bare patches.

If you are growing plants in a jar with the lid closed, the glass may occasionally cloud up with condensation. If it does, open the lid for a few minutes until it clears.

5 Pour water gently into the jar until the soil is wet right through. If you leave the jar open, it will dry out and you will need to water the soil regularly, but if you close the lid, it will stay damp and the plants will grow in their own mini ecosystem.

Rain boot bulbs

Have you grown out of your rain boots again or have you got a hole in one that lets in the rain? Not to worry—old rain boots needn't be thrown away. You can plant them with bulbs in the fall (autumn) to make some colorful planters. Three different types of flowers will come up one after the other to give you exciting surprises for weeks on end.

You will need

A pair of old rain (wellington) boots

Warm soapy water

Acrylic paint pens (if the boots are plain)

Clean gravel or small stones

Potting mix (compost)

2 tulip bulbs

2 daffodil bulbs

8 crocus bulbs

1 Ask an adult to drill a few holes in the soles of an old pair of rain boots. Now wash them on the outside with warm, soapy water. If they are patterned boots, you can get straight on with planting, but if they are plain, when they are dry, use the acrylic pens to decorate them with patterns, pictures, or even a special message.

2 Fill the bottom "foot" section of the first boot with gravel or small stones. This will help the boot stand up and also allow extra water to drain away after heavy rain or a good watering. Put some potting mix on top of the gravel, making sure that you still have a space about 6 inches (15 cm) deep for planting.

3 Put in one tulip and one daffodil bulb, making sure that their pointed ends are facing upward. Cover these over with potting mix, leaving a 2-inch (5-cm) gap at the top of the boot.

4 Plant four crocus bulbs on top of the potting mix, then add more potting mix until the bulbs are covered. Firm it down with your fingers, and add more until the boot is almost full to the top. Plant up the other rain boot in the same way, water both boots well, and then put them somewhere sunny.

5 Check the boots every few days to make sure that the potting mix doesn't dry out and water them if you need to. Watch for the first green shoots to appear in the spring!

Stop-motion bean pot

Ever wondered what happens to seeds after you've planted them in the ground? Now you can find out with these stop-motion bean pots. They will show you the stages of germination and you will be rewarded with a bean plant ready to put in the garden.

You will need

Newspaper

A cardboard tube

Sticky tape

Potting mix (compost)

A clear plastic pint-sized beaker

Colored paper napkins

Pole/Runner or green (climbing French) bean seeds. Instead of runner beans you could grow other types of beans—French beans, fava (broad) beans, or borlotti beans. Only climbing beans will need a cane for support

A small pitcher (jug)

A hand trowel

Bamboo cane

A watering can

1 Place the cardboard tube end down on a double layer of newspaper. Now gather up the newspaper around the tube and secure it with sticky tape. It doesn't have to be neat but one end of the tube must be sealed.

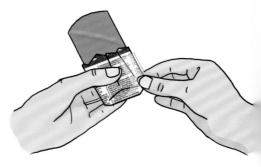

2 Carefully fill the tube with some potting mix, making sure that you firm it down inside the tube as you go (but don't push it through the paper end!). Place the tube in the plastic beaker and stuff paper napkins in the space between the tube and the sides of the beaker.

Be a SCIENTIST—WATCH how seeds GROW!

3 Use your finger to make a hole about 1½ inches (4 cm) deep in the potting mix. Plant a bean seed in the hole, cover it over with more potting mix, and then firm it down. Try not to spill any potting mix over the side of the tube.

4 Push another bean seed about 1½ inches (4 cm) down the side of the beaker between the beaker and the napkin so that you can see it clearly from the outside.

5 With a small pitcher (jug), slowly add water to the tube and beaker so that the potting mix and napkins are both damp.

6 After two days, push another bean down the side of the beaker but a little further along. Keep doing this every two days until you have 6–8 seeds around your pot. Keep the potting compost and napkins damp. Watch the beans begin to germinate one by one and then, as you turn the beaker around, you will be able to see the whole germination process unfold from start to finish.

7 When the central bean has grown two large leaves and you are certain that there will be no more frosts, take the whole cardboard tube carefully out of the beaker. Find a warm sunny spot in your yard or garden, dig a hole that is as deep as the tube, and place the tube into it. Fill the hole with soil around the tube and firm it down with your hands. The tube will rot away as the bean grows. Water it well.

8 Push a garden cane into the soil beside the bean plant—the plant will twine itself around the cane as it grows, but you might want to help it to start climbing by tying it to the cane using a figure eight knot (see page 13). Remember, beans are thirsty plants so keep it well watered.

Herb head flowerpots

Make a mini herb garden for the kitchen windowsill and all you budding chefs can experiment with different flavors when you're helping with the cooking. Line up the flowerpots and paint a row of different faces, then grow some crazy, but tasty, hairstyles!

You will need

Acrylic or matte latex (emulsion) paint in assorted colors

A paintbrush

Terra-cotta flowerpots

Varnish (optional)

A few small stones

Potting mix (compost)

Herb seeds—try basil, parsley, chives, cress, or use small plants like rosemary or thyme

1 Paint a face shape onto the front of the flowerpot. Make sure the face goes all the way up to the top edge of the pot. Let it dry.

2 Decorate the face shape with some eyes, a nose, and a mouth, even a pair of glasses or some clothes if you like (remember—no hair!). When the paint has dried, you can give the pot a coat of varnish to make the paint more hard-wearing, but you don't have to.

3 Place a few small stones at the bottom of the pot to help it to drain and then carefully fill it up with some potting mix until it is about three-quarters full.

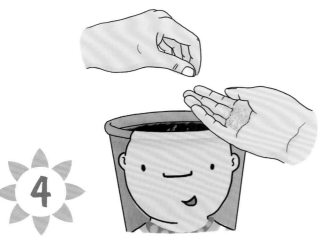

4 Sprinkle some herb seeds on the surface. If you are using cress seeds you do not need any more potting mix on top. For other herbs, sprinkle on a very thin covering of potting mix. Place the pots on saucers on a sunny windowsill.

5 Water your pots regularly but don't let the soil get too wet. Watch as the seedlings begin to grow and turn into hair. Give the pots a haircut when you need some herbs!

Miniature garden

You can make a miniature garden in all sorts of containers, as long as there are some holes in the bottom and you have enough room to be creative. This garden is made in a metal mixing bowl and uses lots of alpine plants, which are naturally tiny and so make perfect trees and bushes to decorate your miniature plot. You can buy them from a garden center.

You will need

A shallow metal mixing bowl, 10 inches (24 cm) in diameter

Gravel or small stones and potting mix (compost)

A selection of alpine plants, such as Hebe 'Maori Gem,' Hebe 'Green Globe,' and Sedum spathulifolium 'Cape Blanco'

Baby sempervivums

A watering can

36 yellow popsicle (lollipop) sticks (you could paint plain ones)

PVA glue

25 green popsicle (lollipop) sticks

Strong scissors

Card

A short piece of string

Thin twigs or canes

A thin piece of material

Mini clothes pins

Thin sticks or twigs

Moss (real or sisal)

A small open shell

1 Ask an adult to drill or puncture five or six holes in the base of your mixing bowl. Put a layer of gravel or small stones in the bottom to stop the potting mix blocking the holes. Add some potting mix and then plant your alpine plants, leaving space for your path, shed, vegetable garden, and washing line. Fill around the plants with potting mix and give them a good watering.

2 To make the sides of the shed, take seven yellow sticks and line them up. Cut a yellow stick in half and glue the two pieces across the width of the first seven. Place something heavy on top until they have stuck firmly. Repeat to make the other side of the shed. Make the ends of the shed the same way but arrange the sticks so that they rise up at the center. (As the sides will be pushed into the potting mix it doesn't matter that the ends aren't even along the bottom.)

3 To make the door, cut the ends off three green sticks with strong scissors and glue them onto the front of the shed. When fully dry, push all four sections into the potting mix so that they form the shed.

4 To make the roof, cut a square of card that is just larger than the top of the shed. Score a line down the middle and bend it in half. Using scissors, cut ten green sticks so that they are slightly longer than one side of the card and stick them on with glue. Repeat this for the other side.

5 Place the roof on top of the shed, bending it down to match the ends. Finally, stick on two green sticks with glue, just slightly longer than the roof, to cover the spine of the card.

6 To make the gate, line up another three yellow sticks with gaps between them. Cut a fourth stick into three equal pieces and glue one across the top, one across the bottom and one diagonally between them. Put a weight on top while it dries and then gently push the gate into position in the potting mix.

A GARDEN fit for a FAIRY

7 To make the washing line, tie the piece of string between two thin sticks or twigs. Push the sticks into the potting mix so that the line is pulled taut. Cut a small piece of thin material to hang like washing on the line and attach it using the mini clothes pins.

8 Break small sections of twig to form the edge of the path from the gate to the shed. Fill the central section with gravel. Push in some thin sticks to make pretend supports for climbing beans and place the baby sempervivums in rows to look like cabbages or lettuces in the vegetable garden.

9 Fill around any bare areas with moss to look like grass. Add an upside-down shell to form a mini birdbath or small pond. Fill this carefully with water from a pitcher (jug).

You can use miniature furniture and figures or small toys to add more features to your garden.

10 Place your miniature garden in a bright sunny place and don't water it too much—alpine plants like to be quite dry.

Cress caterpillar

This green hairy caterpillar will look great on your windowsill and, even better, it will grow delicious cress that you can snip off and add to salads or sandwiches. This one only has three segments—use a 12-egg carton for a six-segment caterpillar if you really enjoy cress.

You will need

Scissors

An egg carton (half-dozen size)

Green poster paint

Paintbrush

A small bowl

Green food coloring

3 eggshell halves

Paper towel

Modeling clay

A sharp pencil

3 green pipe cleaners

1 black pipe cleaner

A pair of googly craft eyes

PVA glue

Absorbent cotton (cotton wool)

Cress seeds (or you could try mustard)

A small plate

1 Cut an egg carton base in half lengthwise and trim down the sides. Paint one half green, inside and out, with the poster paint and let it dry. This will be your caterpillar's body.

2 Fill the bowl with water, add a few drops of green food coloring, and lower in the three eggshell halves. Leave them for about thirty minutes to turn green and then take them out and let them dry on some paper towels.

CREEPY CRAWLY cress caterpillars!

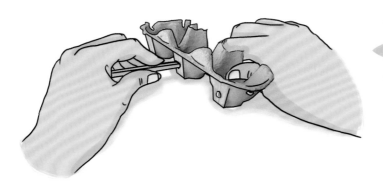

3 Put a ball of modeling clay inside one segment of the egg carton and, using a sharp pencil, poke a hole into the clay through each side for the caterpillar's legs. Do the same for the other two segments (six holes for six legs) and make two holes at the front for the antennae.

4 Thread the three green pipe cleaners through from one side of the carton to the other. Make sure that the legs on each side are the same length, and then bend them into leg shapes.

5 Thread the black pipe cleaner through both holes in the front of the egg carton so that the antennae are the same length, and then bend them upward. Glue the googly eyes onto the front of the caterpillar.

6 Put the dried eggshell halves into the spaces along the caterpillar's back. Dip balls of absorbent cotton (cotton wool) into a bowl of clean water and place one in each eggshell.

7 Empty some cress seeds onto a small plate, take a pinch, and carefully sprinkle the seeds all over the damp absorbent cotton. You should see the cress seeds begin to germinate within a day and your crop of little cress plants will be ready to cut and eat within 3–5 days.

Keep a small pitcher (jug) of water by the caterpillar and add a little to the eggshells every day to ensure that the absorbent cotton does not dry out.

Edible flower colander

Have you ever eaten flowers? Here is your chance to try! This project uses a simple piece of kitchen equipment—a colander—as a container to grow bright and cheerful flowers that you can then add to salads or sandwiches. You can also freeze the petals in ice cubes to bring color to summer drinks.

You will need

A colander or strainer (larger sizes work best)

A thick plastic bag, such as an old potting-mix bag

Scissors

Potting mix (compost)

1 pot marigold (Calendula officinalis)

2–3 nasturtiums (depending on the size of the colander), or other edible flowers like pansies and violets

A watering can

 **1** First make a liner for the colander. Place the colander upside down on the plastic and draw a circle which is about 3–4 inches (8–10 cm) wider than the colander all the way round. Cut it out and then use the scissors to cut a few slits in the center that will let water drain through.

2 Put the plastic circle inside the colander and then half-fill it with potting mix. If the plastic liner sticks up above the edge of the colander, trim it away carefully so that it looks neat.

FLOWERS you can EAT!

Although you can buy nasturtiums and pot marigolds from the garden center, they are easy to grow from seed (see page 12).

3 Gently remove the pot marigold from its container. To do this, hold one hand across the top of the pot, with your fingers around the plant, and turn the pot upside down. Tap the bottom of the pot until the plant comes out. Place the marigold in the center of the colander.

4 Remove the nasturtiums from their pots in the same way as you did for the pot marigold, and then space them evenly around the edge of the colander.

5 Use some more of the potting mix to fill in the spaces between the pot marigold and the nasturtiums, firming down well as you go.

6 Water the plants well. Place the colander outside your window where there is plenty of sun but remember not to let the potting mix dry out. In dry weather, you may need to water it every day. Remember that the best time to water your plants is either early in the morning or in the evening.

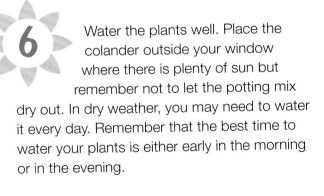

Chapter 3
The Outdoors Indoors

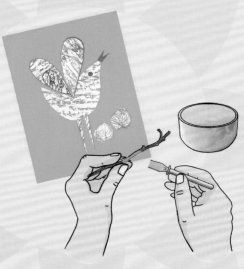

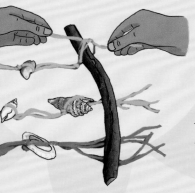

Nature stones

Going for a nature walk gives everyone a great excuse to get out of the house. Next time you go, pick up some natural treasures along the way (an egg carton makes a good collecting box to keep your special finds safe). When you get home, press them into clay to make fossil-like patterns and textures.

You will need

Natural objects, such as seed pods, shells, leaves, and flowers

Block of oven-bake modeling clay

A knife

Flat baking sheet

Oven mitt

1 Go for a nature walk and collect lots of different items that might make interesting prints in the clay. Look for raised patterns and clear outlines—shells are perfect and seed pods and dried cones often have interesting textures. Remember that the natural objects you choose will need to be strong enough to be pressed into a ball of clay.

2 Cut your clay into smaller pieces and roll each piece into a smooth egg-sized ball between your hands.

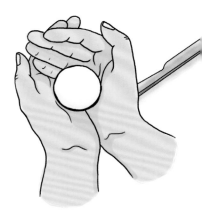

3 Press each item into your clay ball to create a clear print. If something doesn't work well, roll your ball smooth again and try something different. Place the ball on a baking sheet.

4 Ask an adult to help you bake the nature stones in the oven according to the manufacturers' instructions on the package of clay.

Discover NATURE'S amazing PATTERNS

Shell wind chime

Do you always come back from the beach with a pail of shells and then not know what to do with them? Here is something you can make— a wind chime. Hang it in the garden, in a window, or even as an indoor mobile, and listen to the gentle clink of shells in the breeze.

You will need

Colored raffia or ribbon

Scissors

Shells—big ones make louder chimes

A long stick or twig for hanging

1 To make one strand, cut two lengths of raffia about 18 inches (45 cm) long. Tie them together with a knot about 2¼ inches (6 cm) from one end.

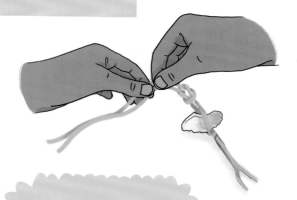

2 Put a shell between the raffia pieces, tight against the knot, and tie another knot above it so that the shell is held tightly between the two knots (a reef knot is a good knot for this, see page 11). Leave a space and then knot the raffia together again and tie in another shell.

Other beachcombing finds, such as small pebbles or pieces of worn, smooth glass in jewel colors, would also make a pretty wind chime full of seaside memories.

3 Tie in some more shells, spacing them evenly along the strand, leaving about 4 inches (10 cm) free at the end. Once the final shell is knotted in place, tie a knot about 2 inches (5 cm) above the last shell.

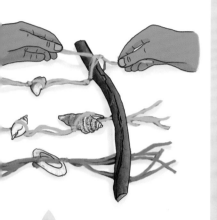

4 Make up two more strands in the same way, using different-colored raffia. Tie the separate strands onto the stick, spacing them evenly. Hang them so the shells knock against each other when they swing. Trim the ends of the raffia.

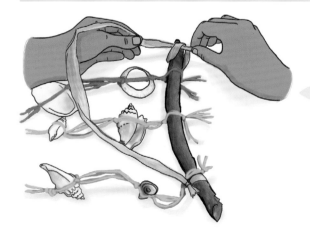

5 Tie a piece of raffia to each end of the stick to make a loop for hanging.

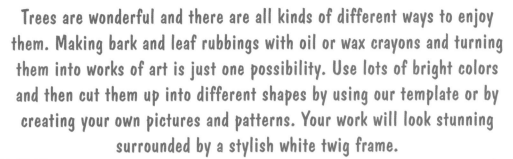

Bark rubbing picture and twig frame

Trees are wonderful and there are all kinds of different ways to enjoy them. Making bark and leaf rubbings with oil or wax crayons and turning them into works of art is just one possibility. Use lots of bright colors and then cut them up into different shapes by using our template or by creating your own pictures and patterns. Your work will look stunning surrounded by a stylish white twig frame.

You will need

Bark rubbings, leaves, and twigs from a local park or wood

A plastic wallet containing lots of pieces of thin white paper

Oil pastels or wax crayons in assorted colors

A bag for collecting leaves and twigs

White or plain wooden frame

White acrylic paint

Paintbrush

PVA glue

Colored paper for background

Scissors

Bird template on page 126, tracing paper, and pencil (optional)

Glue stick

1 First collect your bark rubbings. You'll need to find a place with lots of different trees with different patterns and textures of bark, such as a local park or wood. Choose a tree for your first rubbing. Remove the paper wrapping from around a crayon or pastel. Put a sheet of thin white paper over the bark. Hold it firmly with one hand and rub over it using the long side of the crayon.

2 Make lots of different rubbings of different trees in different colors and place them carefully back in the wallet when you have finished each one. Collect some small leaves and twigs and put them in the bag to take home.

3 At home, start by preparing the frame. Paint your twigs all over with white acrylic paint and let them dry. If you have a wooden frame, give your frame a couple of coats of white paint, too. Allow the first coat to dry before painting the second coat.

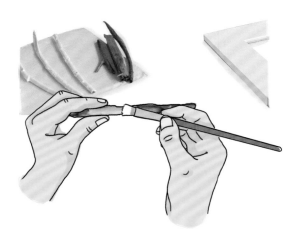

4 When the second coat is dry, arrange the twigs all around the frame and glue them in place. Put aside to dry.

5 While your paint and glue are drying, you can get on with the artwork. First, trace around the backing piece for the frame onto your colored paper and cut it out to make the background.

6 Now make some leaf rubbings. Put the leaves on the table so the bumpy veins face upward. Use a clean piece of white paper and rub over the leaves with the side of a green crayon and then cut out the leaf shapes.

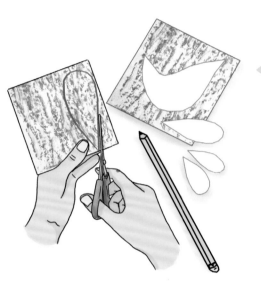

7 Trace the template on page 126 and cut different-colored shapes from the bark rubbings to make up the bird—cut out a body, wings, legs, beak, and eyes.

8 Arrange the bird pieces on the colored background paper and glue in place. Draw in an eye with a crayon. To finish, glue a small twig beneath the bird's feet and add the paper leaves to the end. Put the finished picture in the frame.

Leaf picture frame

When you go for a walk in the fall (autumn), take a bag and make a collection of your favorite leaves. Choose the brightest colors and the most perfect leaves to take home, then use them to make this very special picture frame.

You will need

....

A felt-tipped pen

A large paper plate

Scissors

Card

A sharp pencil and modeling clay

4 split pins

String

A selection of leaves

PVA glue

A paintbrush

2 large dinner plates

Coloring pencils

1 Find a plastic bowl or something round which fits in the middle of your paper plate. Position it in the center and draw around it. Use scissors to cut out this circle carefully—make a hole in the middle and cut out from that, so that you don't cut across the plate. You will end up with a circular frame.

2 Cut out three small leaf-shapes, about 1¾ inches (4 cm) long, from a piece of card—you could draw around real leaves to help. These are retainers to hold your picture in the frame. Make holes in the bottom of each card leaf by pushing the sharp pencil through the card. Push it into the ball of modeling clay to stop it damaging the table. In the same way, make three holes spaced evenly around the inside edge of the paper plate frame.

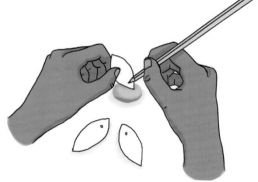

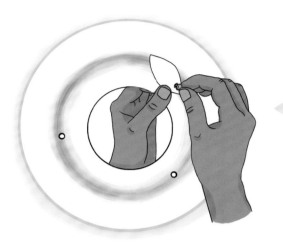

3 On the back of the plate, push a split pin through each of the leaf retainers and the paper plate, and open out the pin on the front side of the frame.

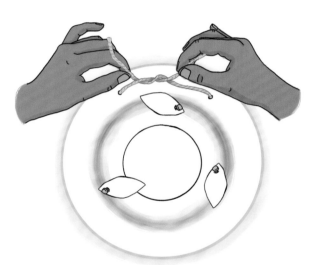

4 Using the pencil and modeling clay, make another two holes at the top of the frame and thread through a piece of string. Tie the ends together to make a loop to hang the picture up.

5 Now sort out your leaves and decide how to arrange them on the frame. Using a paintbrush, carefully paint glue onto the back of each leaf and stick it to the front of the plate frame. To make sure that the leaves stick well, put the picture frame on a large dinner plate and put another plate on top. Then put something heavy on the top plate and let the frame dry for an hour.

Dilute some PVA glue with a little water and then paint it all over the leaves to make them shiny and less crumbly.

6 Now for some artwork to put in the frame. Draw a circle on a piece of card, just larger than the hole in the frame and cut it out. Draw your picture for framing on this card—draw something special for such a special frame. When you have finished, place it on the back of the frame and twist the leaf retainers around to hold it in place.

Catch a FALLING LEAF and make a WISH!

Leaf print Easter eggs

Have you ever really looked at how many different shapes of leaves there are? Go out into your backyard or a park and see how many different small leaves you can collect, then use the prettiest to make these beautiful decorated eggs. Make them for Easter or any time of year. Ferns and groups of small, delicate leaves work well, and the feathery sprigs of dill and fennel are very pretty.

You will need

Hard-cooked (boiled) white eggs (large eggs or duck eggs work well)

A few sprigs of small leaves, such as ferns, dill, fennel

Old pair of pantyhose (tights)

Elastic bands

Cup and spoon

Food coloring

1 Choose a pretty shaped leaf and lay it on the hard-cooked egg in the position you would like. Cut a small section of fabric from an old pair of pantyhose (tights). Position the fabric over the egg and leaf, and gather it together at the back. Make sure the leaf is flat and the fabric is smooth and covers the whole egg.

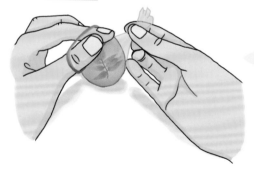

2 Keeping hold of the gathered fabric, wind an elastic band around the gathers tightly to hold everything in place.

3 Fill a cup with water. Add a few drops of food coloring to the cup and stir to mix well. Lower the egg into the cup. Leave for at least ten minutes for the color to take and then check if it is dark enough. If you want a stronger color, use more coloring and leave the egg in the cup for longer. The stronger the color the more clearly you will see the leaf pattern.

When the color is strong enough, lift the egg out using the gathered knot. Carefully remove the elastic band, fabric, and leaf to reveal the leaf pattern. Let it dry before you display it.

If you want to keep your eggs to display the following year, you will have to blow them first (see page 10).

Butterfly shell magnets

Next time you are at the beach see if you can find some complete two-sided shells (be careful with them—they can break apart very easily). You can turn these two-sided shells into pretty butterfly fridge magnets. Don't worry if you can't find any, as you can stick two similar shells next to each other but you may need a larger-sized magnet to attach them to.

You will need

Shells (our picture shows cockle shells but mussels and other double-sided shells would work too)

Acrylic paint in white and assorted colors

Small paintbrush

Small magnets

PVA glue

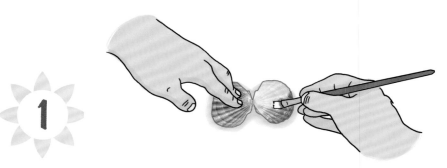

1 Wash the shells in hot, soapy water and dry them, being careful not to break them apart. When completely dry, give the shells a coat of white paint. Let them dry.

2 Paint butterfly wings or a simple pattern on each side of the shell. Try to make the patterns on the two sides symmetrical.

Turn SHELLS into BUTTERFLIES!

3

Once you are happy with the wing pattern, carefully paint the body of the butterfly between the shells and add the antennae.

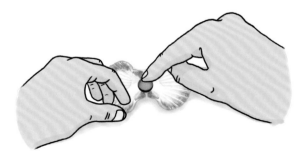

4

When the paint is dry, stick the magnet to the join on the back of the shells with a small dot of glue. Let it dry before attaching to your refrigerator or bulletin board.

Leaf and flower paper

There is something very special about handmade paper but it is easy to make. Different types of scrap paper will make different colors and textures of paper and you can decorate it with leaves, seeds, and flowers in every season. Make the paper into notebooks, bookmarks, or gift tags.

You will need

Scrap paper, such as newspaper, tissue paper, paper bags, computer print outs

Blender

Water

Dish-washing bowl

Embroidery frame

Piece of cheesecloth (muslin) or tulle fabric

Flat leaves, flowers, and seeds

Spoon

Old bath towel

Hole punch (optional)

Ribbon (optional)

1 Start by making a paper pulp. Tear up some scraps of paper into small pieces and put them in a blender until it is half full. Pour in enough water so that the blender is three-quarters full. Ask an adult to help you to whizz the mixture until you have a pulp.

2 Pour the paper pulp into a large bowl, such as a dish-washing bowl. Add two pitchers (jugs) of water, approximately 3½ pints (2 liters), and mix it all around with your hands. It's very messy!

BEAUTIFUL handmade PAPER

3 Separate the two sections of the embroidery frame. Lay a piece of fine fabric, such as cheesecloth (muslin) or tulle, over the smaller section and measure and cut a square of fabric approximately 1¼ inches (3 cm) larger than the frame.

4 With the cheesecloth square over the smaller section, place the larger section of the embroidery frame over the smaller one but don't push it right down. Leave it slightly raised so that there is a rim around the cloth to hold the paper pulp. When it is in position tighten the screw at the side to hold it in place.

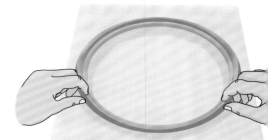

5 Now for the fun bit! Swish your hands around in the water so that the pulp is evenly mixed. Dip the frame down into the pulp, away from your body, and lower it into the water at an angle.

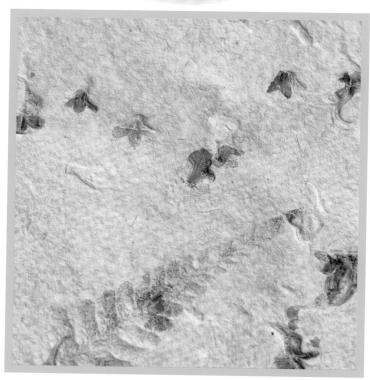

6 Straighten the frame under the water and then slowly bring it out flat. Let the water drip through. Rest the frame on the side of the bowl and arrange your leaves, flowers, or seeds on top. Pour some of the pulp mixture over the flowers and leaves using a spoon.

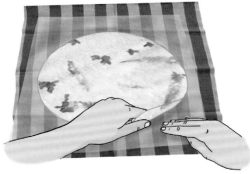

7 Gently place the frame on a towel, undo the screw, and take the frame off the cheesecloth. If you have some more cheesecloth you can now make another sheet of paper. Let the finished paper dry on the cheesecloth for several hours or overnight. The next day it should be dry and you can carefully peel the paper away from the cloth.

8 To make a notebook, cut out some rectangles from the paper circle to make a front and back cover. Cut some plain paper the same size for the inside of the book. Punch holes through all the layers, thread some ribbon through, and tie together. Use any trimmings to make gift labels.

Pine cone animals

Pine cones come in all shapes and sizes and are fun to collect, but whatever can you do with them? Here is one answer—make a family of cute animals decorated with felt ears, pompom eyes, and pipe-cleaner tails! We have shown you how to make a mouse and some owls but you can use your imagination to decide what kind of animal each of your pine cones will become.

You will need

Pencil and paper

Scissors

Scraps of colored felt

PVA glue

Pipe cleaners

Pine cones

Miniature pompoms

1 Draw an ear shape on paper and cut it out with scissors to make a template. Place the template on the felt and draw around it. Repeat to make a second ear.

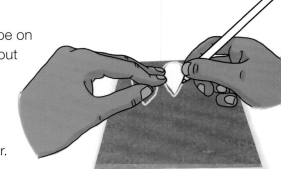

2 Carefully cut out the ears. Pinch each one in half and put a dab of glue inside the bottom end of the fold to form a pleat. Hold them tightly as they dry. Let them dry completely.

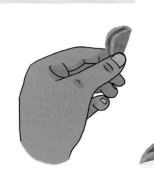

3 Cut a length of pipe cleaner about 4 inches (10 cm) long and wind it around your finger to make a curly tail.

4

Bend up the end of the pipe cleaner by about ½ inch (1 cm). Use a dab of glue at the base of the pine cone to attach the bent up part of the tail. Press down gently to make sure the tail is stuck firmly and let it dry completely.

5 Put a small dab of glue on the base of the ears and push them in place between the layers of the pine cone. Use two miniature pompoms for the eyes and glue them just below the ears to finish.

6 To make a mother owl and her baby, use one large and one small pine cone. Cut the wings from brown felt, use a triangle of red felt for the beak, pompoms for the eyes, and short lengths of pipe cleaners, bent in half, for feet.

Nature journal

Making a nature journal is a great way to record what you see out in the countryside. Show how much you care about nature by making your journal out of reused materials, like cardboard from a box. When you go out, draw pictures and make notes about what you see and take home small, interesting finds in the pocket.

You will need

Scrap paper (US letter or A4 size)

Brown cardboard carton or box

Ruler and pencil

Scissors

Colored paper

Hole punch

Raffia or string made from natural fibers, like sisal or jute

An old envelope (a colored one from a birthday card would look nice)

Dried seeds or leaves for decoration

PVA glue and glue stick

To make your journal even more eco-friendly, use scrap computer print out paper that has only been printed on one side, for the pages.

1 Take a piece of scrap paper. Fold down the top left corner to the bottom edge (so that the left edge lines up with the bottom edge). Crease along the fold to make a triangle. Cut along the side of the triangle. Open up the triangle and you have a square template.

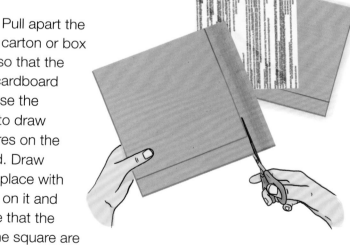

2 Pull apart the carton or box so that the cardboard lies flat. Use the template to draw two squares on the cardboard. Draw them in a place with no writing on it and make sure that the sides of the square are in line with the ridges in the cardboard. Cut out the squares—ask an adult to help if the cardboard is very thick.

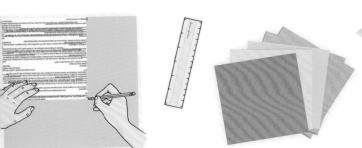

Cut sheets of colored paper to the same size as the cardboard. Use the template to mark where to cut the paper and draw across with a ruler before you cut to be sure the line is straight.

4 Using the hole punch, make two holes on one edge of each square of paper and both cardboard squares. Try to make the holes in the same place on each sheet.

5 Put the paper squares on top of one of the cardboard squares. Put the second cardboard square on the top. Line up all the holes. Cut two pieces of raffia or string about 10 inches (25 cm) long. Thread them through the holes and tie with neat bows to make your journal. Don't tie them too tight or you won't be able to turn the pages.

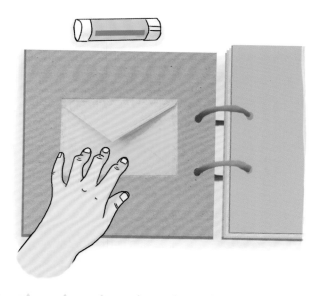

6 Spread glue over the front of the envelope (where the address goes) and stick it to the inside of the front cover.

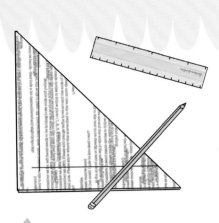

7 Take the template and fold it along the diagonal crease, then measure and draw a line 1 inch (2.5 cm) away from the two straight (not the diagonal) edges. Cut along these lines to make a smaller square template.

An ECO-FRIENDLY notebook

8 Use this to cut out a small plain paper square for the cover of your journal. If you like, write your name and a title on it and stick it in place.

9 Arrange dried seeds or leaves around the cover of your book and stick them down with PVA glue. Put a heavy board or book on top of the journal while the glue dries to make sure they stick firmly.

Chapter 4
Outdoor Crafts and Games

Fruity boats

We usually throw the skins of fruits like melons, oranges, lemons, or mangoes into the compost bin but you could make them into a fleet of little boats to sail on a pond or even in the bath! Make sails of pretty scrap paper with a leaf for a flag and afterward, enjoy eating up the delicious fruit you have scooped out.

1 Ask an adult to help you to cut the fruit in half. Use a spoon to scoop out the flesh and put it into a bowl ready to eat, leaving the skin or peel in one piece. Be careful not to make any holes.

You will need

Fruit with a strong skin such as melons, oranges, grapefruit, mangoes, or avocados

A spoon and bowl

Leafy stalks or twigs

A small piece of modeling clay

Scissors

Scraps of paper or tissue paper

2 Strip off the lower leaves from your stalk or twig, leaving one in place at the top to look like a flag.

3 Cut out a sail from your scraps of paper or tissue. You can make it a rectangle or a triangle. Push the lower end of a twig through the paper sail near the top and then out again further down the sail.

4 Place a small ball of modeling clay in the bottom of the boat. Push the end of the sail twig into the clay—you're ready to launch!

REMEMBER: Always take care near water—never enter water to fetch a boat that has blown out of reach.

Driftwood game

This game is perfect when you are in the woods or park, or at the beach. Simply collect four sticks of a similar length and bind them together to make the board. You could use raffia or string to do this, but why not use nature? Reeds, long grass, or climbing plant vines would work. Tie small sticks together to make the crosses and collect pebbles or shells for the noughts. The aim of the game is to make a line of three noughts or crosses, while trying to block your opponent from doing the same. The first player to get three in a row wins.

You will need

4 sticks, about 16 inches (40 cm) long

Something to bind them together (long grass, climbing plants, raffia, or string)

10 short, thin sticks

5 pebbles

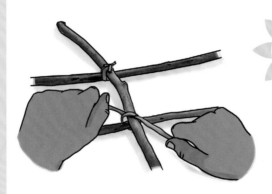

1 Find four sticks that are about the same length and arrange them in a crisscross pattern. Find something that you can use to tie them together and wind it a couple of times around the join of two sticks, tying it with a knot.

 **2** Continue to bind all the sticks together in the same way. If you have a penknife you could use it carefully to trim the ends of your binding.

Why buy **GAMES** when you can **MAKE** your own?

3 Snap thinner lengths of stick into 10 short pieces. Make a cross by taking two sticks and binding them together around the middle.

4 Twist the sticks so they form an "X" shape and tie the binding across the other way to hold it in place, finishing with a knot. Repeat steps 3 and 4 to make four more crosses. Collect your pebbles and you're ready to play!

Twig raft

Who doesn't enjoy messing around with boats and what could be more fun than constructing your own raft to sail on a stream or pond? And just think, the skills you learn here could come in useful if you were ever stranded on a desert island!

You will need

Straight, thin sticks or twigs, such as willow

String

Scissors

A small scrap of sacking (or some thin cardboard)

A leaf

Small ball of modeling clay

1 Break some thin sticks into equal lengths about 8 inches (20 cm) long, or to the size you want. Lay the sticks alongside each other and keep adding more until you are happy with the width of the raft. Measure a length of string to match the width of the raft, double this length and then double it again so it is about four times as wide as the raft. Cut it and then cut two more pieces of string the same length as this one. Fold the first piece of string in half and loop it around the first stick about a quarter of the way along.

2 Twist the string, and then put the next stick beside the first one so that what was the bottom piece of string goes over the next stick and what was the top piece goes under it. Twist it again and add in another stick. Keep doing this until all your sticks are attached. Pull the string tight and finish with a double knot (try a reef knot, see page 11). Trim off the ends.

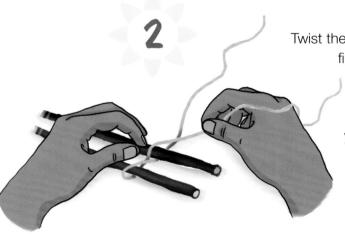

Are you **READY** to face the **RAPIDS?**

3 Take the second piece of string, fold it in half and slide the fold over the first stick, so both ends are on top. Pull it along until it is in the center of the raft. Now take the end which went over the top of the first stick and loop it over the end of the second stick, so that it goes underneath this one, and pull it back to the center. Do the same for the next sticks, always taking the string that was on top and looping it under the next stick—it will end up just like your first string.

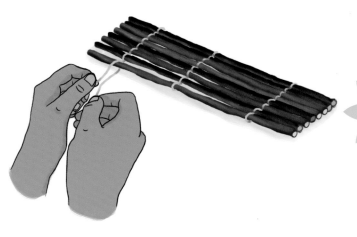

4 When all the sticks are tied in, pull the string tight and finish with a double knot as before. Do the same with the third piece of string, positioning it so that the three strings are evenly spaced.

5 Choose a stick for the mast—not too tall or heavy or the raft will capsize. Cut a rectangle of sacking (or thin card) and push a twig through at the base and out near the top, to form a sail. Push the top of the mast through a leaf to make a flag.

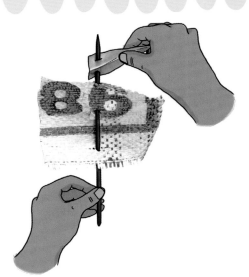

6 To attach the sail to the raft, mold a small ball of modeling clay into a cone shape and push it down firmly onto the center of the raft. Push the mast into the clay.

REMEMBER: Always take care near water—never enter water to fetch a raft that has blown out of reach.

7 Finally, test your raft in the water to make sure it balances correctly. If it tips to one side, add a bit of modeling clay to the opposite side and test it again. If it's still unbalanced, add a little more clay until you get the perfect weight distribution.

Natural garland

This garland is rather like natural bunting—a string of beautiful treasures to decorate your tent, your garden, or your home. Collect leaves, seedpods, flower heads, and anything else that looks interesting. Objects with short stems are the easiest to tie in. Use natural fiber string so that your whole garland will turn to compost when you have finished with it.

You will need

Natural twine or string (jute or sisal)

Scissors

Selection of leaves, seedpods, pine cones, grasses, and rosehips. You could include other berries but you must check first that they are not poisonous. Never pick wild flowers and ask before you pick flowers from the garden.

Colored raffia or string, optional

1 Make a collection of interesting natural objects such as seed heads, colorful leaves, feathers, and pine cones. Each should have a short stem for attaching it to the string.

Make NATURAL bunting

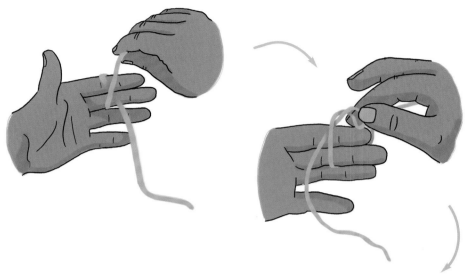

You need to tie each treasure to the string with a slip knot. This sounds complicated but it's easy to do. If you can find someone to show you how, it will be even easier!

2 Cut a piece of twine or string about 40 inches (1 m) long. About 4 inches (10 cm) from one end, wind the string once around your finger and cross the ends. Slide the loop off your finger, hold it in one hand and with the other hand push the long end of string in another loop up through the hole. Take hold of the second loop with one hand and with the other hand pull the two ends so that the first loop tightens around the second one. You have made the first slip knot.

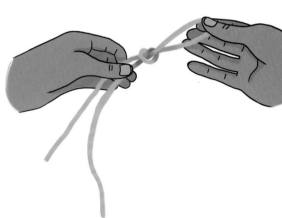

3 Put the stalk of one of your treasures through the loop of the slip knot, pull the two ends and the loop will tighten around the stem, holding it firm.

4 A little further along the twine, tie another slip knot in the same way. Put the stem of your next treasure into the loop and tighten it.

5 Keep going all the way along your twine, adding in as many treasures as you can, but leave 4 inches (10 cm) at the end for tying the garland to a branch or pole. For extra decoration, tie a length of brightly colored raffia or string around the end of each of the treasures, finishing with a bow.

River race game

When you next find a footbridge across a river, remember this traditional game, then take it one step further and turn it into a craft activity. Decorate sticks with leaves, feathers, and stems of grass and race them with your friends or family. Make sure that you only use natural materials that you find outdoors (no plastics) so that you do not pollute the stream or river with anything that will not rot down.

You will need

Sticks

Long blades of grass (you could use raffia if you have some)

Feathers

Leaves

1 Collect a stick for each player, making sure that they are all a similar size. Collect feathers and long thin leaves. Make your collection different from your friend's to help you recognize your own stick.

2 Hold some leaves and feathers around the ends of your stick and wrap long blades of grass around them to hold them in place. Tie the ends in a knot. (This is easier if one person holds and the other wraps and ties.) Make sure that your leaves and feathers are streamlined to make your stick go faster!

3 Add more decoration by wrapping grass around the sticks to make stripes, tying the ends with a knot. You can tie on more leaves and feathers, too—make a design that is easy to identify.

 When everyone has decorated a stick, you are ready to play the game. Stand on a bridge looking upstream so that the water is flowing toward you. On a count of three drop your stick into the water.

5 Race to the other side of the bridge to see whose stick appears first. The first stick to be spotted is the winner. Watch your sticks sail into the distance and then start all over again.

Always take care near water—never go into the water to catch your stick. Never play this on road bridges and always take care when crossing the bridge to watch for your stick.

Ready, steady, GO!

Treasure trail

If you are out camping or have a large garden or wild place to play in, create an adventure for your friends with a treasure trail. Make a map, plus arrows from twigs, and leave pebbles, feathers, or colorful leaves to collect along the way. Put one special prize at the end. Avoid leaving food as a prize, as animals may get to it before the winner does!

You will need

A notebook and pencil

Thick paper

A used wet tea bag

Pen and colored pencils

A bunch of twigs

Raffia or string made of natural fibers (jute or sisal)

Small collections of natural objects (pebbles, feathers, daisies, pine cones—one of each for each of your friends)

A small treat for the treasure

1 First plan out your treasure hunt. Take a notebook and a pencil out to where you want your trail to begin. Find a good starting place, like a tree stump. Mark it on your paper. Decide if you are going to go right, left, or straight on. Mark the direction on your paper, then walk in that direction, counting your paces as you go.

When you reach the next landmark to put on your map—perhaps a tall pine tree or a tumbledown shed—write on your map how many paces you took and draw the landmark. You could give it a pirate name like "Pirate Pete's Pine Tree" or "Hut of Doom."

2 Choose the next direction and start walking again, counting paces to the next landmark and filling in the details on your map. You can mark other things (such as bridges, paths, and rocks) that you pass on the map, too. Keep adding to your trail in this way until you think it is long enough.

3 Go inside and prepare the paper for your real map. You want it to look like an old pirate map so tear the edges roughly and tear off the corners. Make it look even older by dabbing a used wet tea bag all over it to turn it brown and crumpled. Dampen the tea bag if it becomes too dry but make sure that it is not dripping. Let the paper dry.

4 Now carefully copy your treasure trail from your notebook onto the tea-bagged paper. (Spelling doesn't matter because pirates who buried treasure couldn't spell!) At each landmark on the map write a note to tell your friends what to collect there. For example, "Pick up a pebble here" or "Find a feather under the ferns."

5 Now make twig arrows to show the directions on the trail. Take a twig and lay a shorter twig at an angle at one end of it. Bind them together with raffia or string, finishing with a knot. Place another short twig at the tip of the first to make an arrow shape and bind it on as before. Make one of these to put at the beginning and enough extra to put one down after each landmark on the trail.

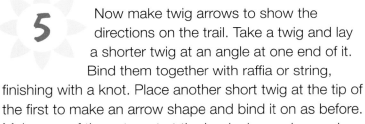

6 To show your friends that they have arrived at the right place, you will need to mark it with a cross. Take two twigs of a similar length and lay one over the other to form a cross shape. Bind them together in the middle, with the string, making a cross shape between the twigs. Finish with a knot. Make one of these for each landmark on the trail.

7 When you have made everything, take a basket with your arrows, crosses, special tokens, prize, and map and set up the trail. Go to your starting position and put down one arrow showing in which direction your friends need to start walking. Lay it on the ground or wedge it in a tree.

8 Put a cross at the first special landmark on your trail. Leave a pile of whatever it is your friends must collect there. Now position the next arrow pointing in the direction of the next landmark. Keep going until you reach the end.

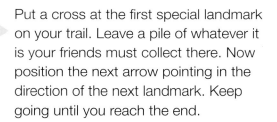

9 At the last landmark, place the prize under a pile of leaves or stones with a big cross on the top. Now go back to the beginning and walk the trail, following the map, to check that everything is where it needs to be. Give your friends the map and see if they can find the treasure!

Teddies' wigwam

Your teddies can camp too with this cute little wigwam. It is quick and easy to make and doesn't require any sewing at all. When you have made it, you can put in piles of dry grass for beds and make stools and tables with sticks and stones. Have a pretend campfire outside the entrance.

You will need

4 sticks about 27 inches (70 cm) long

A piece of fabric, about 20 x 47 inches (50 x 120 cm)

String

Ribbon, twine, or raffia

Scissors

1 Find some long straight sticks with no side shoots on them—they need to be longer than the width of your fabric. You may need to break the side shoots off or ask an adult to help you cut them off.

2 Find some flat soft ground to make your teddies' camp. Push the four sticks into the ground to make the corners of a square. The sides of the square should be about two hand spans apart—a bit more if you have very small hands!

3 Cut a long piece of string. Gather the top ends of the sticks together and wrap the string around them a few times to hold them firm. Finish with a tight knot (see page 11).

4 Wrap the fabric around the frame, gathering it around the top. Hold the fabric in place by wrapping the ribbon around the top and finish with a bow.

5 Cut two smaller pieces of string. Twist the wigwam fabric around so the opening is in the middle of two sticks. Tie the bottom corners of the fabric onto the sticks to make the opening to the wigwam.

Pebble games

You won't need to take any store-bought games to the beach with these pebbly game ideas. The games are best played with two or more people but you can have lots of fun playing them on your own, too. Remember, don't take the pebbles home with you.

You will need

....

Large smooth, flat pebbles

Pebbles to throw

Pebble skittles

1 Collect two sorts of pebbles: first, some large, smooth flat ones to make the skittles. Then collect some smaller round ones for throwing.

2 Make three towers by piling 5–10 of the flat pebbles on top of each other.

3 Stand by the pebble towers, take three large paces away from them, and draw a line in the sand to mark your throwing position.

4   Each player has a pile of throwing pebbles. The players stand behind the line and take it in turns to throw pebbles at the skittles to knock them over.

5   Who can be the first to knock down a skittle? Invent your own rules and scoring system. When you have knocked them all down build them up and start again.

Take AIM and THROW

Pebble towers

1 For a change from knocking down the pebble skittles, try making them into even taller pebble towers instead. Who can make the tallest tower? Or be artistic and see who can make the most beautiful pebble sculpture.

Pebble bowls

1 Find a big stone and put it on some flat damp sand. Draw a circle around it in the sand. Draw another circle around the first one. Draw two more circles to make a target. Number the circles 1, 2, 3, and 4 by drawing numbers in the sand.

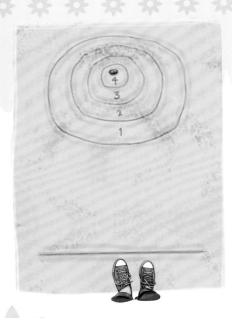

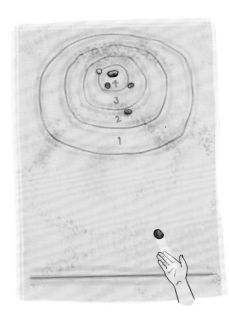

2 Draw a line in the sand a little way from the target. This is the throwing line.

3 Give each player five pebbles and get them to stand behind the throwing line. Each player throws a pebble to try and hit the target. If they hit the big stone they score 10. For throws that miss, they score according to the circle they land in (1, 2, 3, or 4 points).

Never throw stones toward people. Make sure there is no one behind the skittles or bowls target when you throw.

4 Make a score card by drawing in the sand. Who will score the most points?

Beach monsters

When you go to the beach, go beachcombing and collect pebbles, shells, bits of driftwood, feathers, and seaweed—then make them into a crazy sea monster! You can do the same in the woods, using fallen leaves, twigs, seedpods, grasses, and stones to make ferocious woodland monsters lurking behind trees. The colored leaves in the fall (autumn) make wonderful snake or dragon scales.

You will need

Pebbles
Shells
Seaweed
Driftwood

1 Walk along the beach and collect materials for your creatures. Collect pebbles, shells, seaweed, and anything that you think looks useful, but natural materials are best.

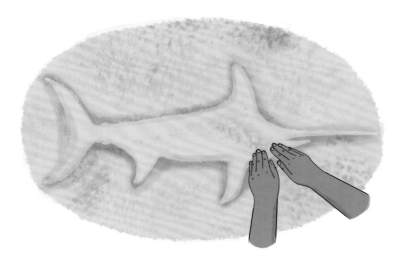

2 Pile up sand to make a head or body shape, patting the sand to make it smooth. Any shape or size will work so try some little tiny heads and great big ones, too.

3 Make some glaring eyes in the head by pushing in some of your beachcombing finds—add pupils to the eyes and eyebrows to add expression.

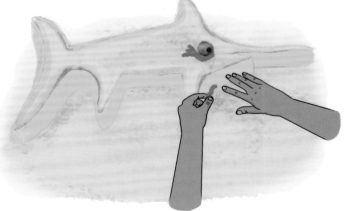

4 Will your monster have a nose? How can you make it? Use shells or driftwood or round pebbles for nostrils or spiky horns. Use shells or little pebbles pushed into the sand to make teeth—try adding ferocious fangs, too!

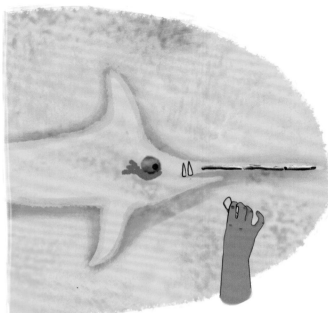

5 Add seaweed, feathers, or shells to make mad hair, crazy crowns, or hats on your sea creatures. Make a long body with pebbles or driftwood.

6 Finally, if you have a camera, take a photo of your creation!

Make a MONSTER of the DEEP

Conker creatures

A walk in the fall (autumn) is the perfect opportunity to gather seeds to make funny conker (chestnut) creatures. Use conkers and acorns for the heads and bodies and add smaller seeds or leaves for decoration. Little twigs make great arms and try sycamore seeds for flappy feet.

You will need

Conkers (chestnuts), acorns, seeds, and leaves

Small twigs for the arms

Modeling clay (plasticine) or fast-drying PVA glue

1 Go for a woodland walk and collect conkers, acorns, and other seeds and leaves.

2 Take a piece of modeling clay and stick it onto a conker or acorn. Push another conker or acorn into it to make a head, or glue the pieces together if you have some PVA glue.

3 To make the feet, stick a piece of modeling clay onto the bottom of the body and push two seeds into it. Flatten the bottom of the modeling clay so that your creature will stand up.

4 Break a twig into two small pieces for the arms and attach them onto either side of the body with a blob of modeling clay.

5 To make a collar or a necklace, push seeds into the modeling clay between the head and the body. For a fancy collar, push the stems of a few small leaves into the modeling clay.

6 To add buttons, put a tiny blob of modeling clay or glue on the body and stick seeds in place. Now make some more for a whole family of woodland folk!

Templates

Trace these templates for the bark rubbing picture (see page 72) and use them to cut out different colored shapes from the bark rubbings to make up the bird—cut out a body, wings, legs, beak, and eyes.

Suppliers and resources

Although you'll collect lots of materials from the outdoors for these projects, here are some links to places that sell craft and gardening materials and equipment.

US

A C Moore
www.acmoore.com

Arizona Pottery
www.arizonapottery.com

Avant Gardens
www.avantgardensne.com

Backyard Gardener
www.backyardgardener.com

Craft Site Directory
www.craftsitedirectory.com
Useful online resource.

Create For Less
www.createforless.com

Gardener's Supply Company
www.gardeners.com

Hobby Lobby
www.hobbylobby.com

Irish Eyes Garden Seeds
www.irisheyesgardenseeds.com

Jo-Ann Fabric & Crafts
www.joann.com

KidsGardening
www.kidsgardening.org
Part of The National Gardening Association.

Loose Ends
www.looseends.com
Craft materials including dried flowers and foliage, raffia ribbon, ribbons, and ties.

Lowe's Home Centers
www.lowes.com

Michaels
www.michaels.com

Nichols Garden Nursery
www.nicholsgardennursery.com
Every kind of vegetable seed imaginable, as well as herb plants, citrus trees, olive trees, strawberry plants, and gardening supplies and tools.

S&S Worldwide Craft Supplies
www.ssww.com

White Flower Farm
www.whiteflowerfarm.com
A wide selection of houseplants for the terrarium project.

UK

Baker Ross
www.bakerross.co.uk
Craft supplies.

B&Q
www.diy.com

Capital Gardens
www.capitalgardens.co.uk

Dan the Gardener
www.danthegardener.co.uk
Useful gardening advice for kids plus colorful, good-quality kids' garden tools.

Early Learning Centre
www.elc.co.uk

Great Little Trading Co.
www.gltc.co.uk
Ready-mixed paint, art folders, and "paint-your-own" kits.

Harrod Horticultural
www.harrodhorticultural.com

Hobbycraft
www.hobbycraft.co.uk

Homebase
www.homebase.co.uk

Homecrafts Direct
www.homecrafts.co.uk

Jekka's Herb Farm
www.jekkasherbfarm.com

John Lewis
www.johnlewis.co.uk

Organic Plants
www.organicplants.co.uk

Parker Dutch Bulbs
www.jparkers.co.uk
Good value source of mail-order bulbs.

Suttons Seeds
www.suttons.co.uk
A special selection of child-friendly seeds that are easy to grow.

West Six Garden Centre
www.w6gc.co.uk

Wilkinsons
www.wilkinsonplus.com

William Sinclair Horticulture
www.william-sinclair.co.uk
Special and general composts, plant foods, soil conditioners, and mulches.

Woolworths
www.woolworths.co.uk

Index

A
animals, conker creatures 123–5
  pine cone 88–9

B
bark 8
bark rubbing picture 72–5
beach monsters 120–2
beans, climbing 38–41, 48–51
bird feeder 20–1
birdbath, pebble 31–3
boats, fruity 96–7
braiding (plaiting) 11
bulbs, in rain (wellington) boots
  46–7
butterfly shell magnets 82–3

C
cardboard containers 9
caterpillar, cress 58–61
clay, modeling 68–9
  for seed bombs 34
climbing bean archway 38–41
clothing, for foraging 8
colander, edible flower 62–5
collecting materials 8–9
  containers 9
conker creatures 123–5
crafting, techniques 10–11
cress caterpillar 58–61

D
driftwood game 98–9
drying flowers 8

E
Easter eggs, leaf print 80–1
egg cartons 9, 58–9
eggs, blowing 10

F
fabric scraps 9
fairy posies 18–19
flowers 8, 15
  edible 62–5
frames, leaf 76–9
  twig 72–5
fruit 9, 14
fruity boats 96–7

G
games, beach monsters 120–2
  driftwood 98–9

pebbles 116–19
river race 108–9
teddies' wigwam 114–15
treasure trail 110–13
garden projects 12–13, 15,
  105–7
gardens, miniature 54–7
garland, natural 105–7
giant's garden 15
glass jars, for terrarium 44–5
glue 10

H
herb head flowerpots 52–3

I
insect hotel 28–30

J
jars, empty 9
journal, nature 90–3

L
leaf and flower paper 84–7
leaf picture frame 76–9
leaves 8

M
marigolds, pot 62–5
materials, collecting 8–9
  gardening 12
miniature gardens 54–7

N
nasturtiums 62–5
natural gardens 15, 105–7
nature journal 90–3
nesting box, wooden 25–7
notebook, nature 90–3
noughts and crosses 98–9

P
paint 10
paper, leaf and flower 84–7
  reused 9
peanut hearts 36–7
pebble birdbath 31–3
pebble bowls 118–19
pebble skittles 116–17
pebble towers 118
pictures, bark rubbing 72–5
  leaf framed 76–9
pine cones 8

animals 88–9
plants 14–15
  care of 13
  fruit and vegetables 14
  poisonous 15
  for pots 15
  scented 15
posies, fairy 18–19
pumpkin, bird feeder 20–1

R
raft, twig 100–3
rain boots, bulbs in 46–7
recycling and reusing 9
reef knot 11
river race 108–9

S
salad bowl garden 14
scissors and knives 10
seed bombs 34–5
seed heads 8
seeds, growing 12–13, 14
shells, butterfly shell magnets
  82–3
  wind chime 70–1
sticks, popsicle (lollipop) 26,
  54–6
stones, nature 68–9
stop-motion bean pots 48–51
string 10, 11

T
templates 126
terrarium, tiny 44–5
treasure trail 110–13
twigs 8, 72–5, 100–3

V
vegetable gardens 14
  wheelbarrow 22–4

W
wellington boots, bulbs in 46–7
wheelbarrow vegetable garden
  22–4
wigwam, teddies' 114–15
wind chime, shell 70–1

✸ Acknowledgments

Key: t = top, c = center, b =
bottom, l = left, r = right

Project makers

Emma Hardy: pp 90–93,
98–99, 104–107, 108–109,
110–113, 114–115, 116–119,
120–122, 123–125
Dawn Isaac: pp 22–24, 28–30,
38–41, 46–47, 48–51,
54–57, 58–61, 62–65, 76–79
Kate Lilley: pp 34–35, 68–69
Catherine Woram/Martyn Cox:
pp 18–19, 20–21, 25–27,
31–33, 36–37, 44–45, 88–89
Clare Youngs: pp 52–53,
70–71, 72–75, 80–81, 82–83,
84–87, 96–97, 100–103

Photography

Carolyn Barber (styling by Liz
Belton): pp 35, 69
Emma Mitchell: pp 1, 7, 13, 16,
23, 29, 30, 39, 41, 42, 47,
49, 50, 55, 56, 59, 61, 63,
64, 77, 78
Debbie Patterson (styling by
Emma Hardy): pp 2, 3, 4, 5b,
66, 91, 93, 94, 99, 104, 107,
109, 111, 115, 117, 118, 119, 121,
123, 125
Claire Richardson (styling by
Clare Youngs): pp 5tc, 6, 8, 9tr,
53, 71, 73, 75, 81, 83, 85, 86,
97, 101, 102
Polly Wreford: pp 5t, 5bc, 9tl,
19, 21, 27, 32, 37, 45, 89